KINGDOM KEYS
for building prosperity

Unmasking some of the lies
Christians believe about money

JANET
NATTA

wildsidepublishing.com

Published by Janet Natta in New Zealand
janetnatta.co.nz | smartmoneyadvice.co.nz

Editing: Elaine Young
Cover design and text layout: Wild Side Publishing
wildsidepublishing.com

Cataloguing in Publication Data:
Title: Kingdom Keys for Building Prosperity

ISBN: 978-0-473-63466-7 (paperback)
      978-0-473-63467-4 (EPUB)

Subjects: Study Aids, Financial Aid, Personal Finance, Business &
Economics, Accounting, Financial, Corporate Finance General, Corporate
Finance Private Equity, Financial Risk Management, Financial Engineering,
Christian, Non-Fiction, New Zealand, Christian Living

First New Zealand printing, July 2022
International listing, Ingram Spark September 2022

Contents

Endorsement

God and money. I love this subject, it's taboo which makes it fun. Good on you Janet for tackling it in this book.

Decades ago we got taught that wealth was wrong, then it seemed that God had a change of heart and the prosperity gospel was on every preacher's lips. Then, suddenly, that was wrong too, then it was ok again, and so on. Meanwhile the reality is that most of us need daily to deal with where money fits in our 'God and Me' stories.

Prosperity, as Janet writes, is of course a Biblical principle and not wrong at all—however expecting it to come and our debt to go just because we wish for it is unrealistic. For my own part, my wealth has grown as I have learned to hear God's voice. Wealth starts with desire (he will advise you on what to desire), followed by organised plans (He's great at step-by-step plans), and then the fun part (He loves fun), following through on those plans.

Mark Holloway. Best Selling Author.
The Freedom Diaries | Cry the Wounded Land
What They Never Told You | 11 DAYS

Introduction

My input into this material comes from a mixture of the work that I do every day as a financial planner and from my heart as a Kingdom citizen.

Getting this material together has been a journey for me. The Holy Spirit had His input ready to go and literally downloaded it in my heart in one afternoon. However, actually putting my part into words has been a three-year journey for me, part of which involved a bit (OK, a lot) of Jonah-like behaviour and a lot of wandering around the same mountain in the wilderness.

Proverbs 16:9 says,

*"In his heart a man plans his course, but the
Lord determines his steps."*

However, Proverbs 16:3 says,

*"Commit to the Lord whatever you do,
and your plans will succeed."*

When I was starting to get serious about this project, I spent a morning in the local Hamilton gardens, seeking God's guidance on what to do, both with this project and with my business. I was led to the start of the book of Nehemiah and the Holy Spirit showed me a blueprint in the very first chapter. Here is what I noticed in verses 1–10.

Step 1: Nehemiah was really distressed and convicted in his heart by something.

Step 2: Nehemiah sought God's face. He spent several days earnestly and wholeheartedly doing this.

Step 3: Nehemiah then:
  a) reminded God of His goodness (worship);
  b) reminded God of His promises;
  c) repented of his own sins and those of his father's house and his people (because sin was a nationwide issue); and
  d) asked for God's favour.

The rest of the book covers off what happened as a result. Nehemiah was successful in the massive undertaking of rebuilding the walls of Jerusalem.

Back then, a city needed walls to protect its citizens from the attack of the enemy. A city with broken walls showed that the people were defeated. The restoration of the walls of Jerusalem was tangible evidence that God was providing for His people. It wasn't EASY. Most things that have a massive impact for the good of the Kingdom of God are not easy. God never promised us "easy". But He did promise us His love and full support—and if we do it His way, we will succeed. Doing it <u>God's way</u> is the key.

If your finances are a city with no walls—if you are defeated and unprotected from the world—you need to take the time to follow Nehemiah's process before you start the journey of rebuilding your defences.

The most "successful" people in the Bible have tended to have a strong, ongoing, two-way relationship with God. If you find it difficult to hear from God, I would encourage you to get hold of a copy of *The Freedom Diaries* by Mark Holloway. This will give you some simple guidelines on how to start a back-and-forth conversation with God.

I try to spend at least an uninterrupted couple of hours with God each week, seeking His wisdom and guidance for my family, my business and my life.

I like to find a quiet café early in the morning, and I sit in the corner with my Bible and my notebook while God and I talk about stuff. Some of God's ideas are a bit (okay, a lot) out of left field, but He did create the universe so I guess that He has some evidence of historical success! I cannot count the number of times that He has saved my bacon by reminding me of words that He has given me. When a crisis hits I go straight to PANIC and start praying (at top volume). Then God says, "Remember that I said..." and I say, "Oh YEAH, I remember that!" Boom... we have a plan.

I have used italics throughout the book to indicate the revelation the Holy Spirit gave me in each area of finances, supported by Scripture (also in italics). I pray that you receive the heart of this message from God for YOUR life.

As you journey to financial success—whatever that looks like for you—please remember that we have to understand HOW

God wants us to live before we can make our plans and have them succeed. That is why we need to seek God's face, and His guidance.

Pastor Suzette Torti once said to me that everyone is born with the spirit of LACK in their lives. Some people pick it up and entertain it, while others rebuke it. If you are honouring (feeding) the spirit of lack, it will continue to manifest in your life.

After you have repented for honouring the spirit of lack, declare the truth of God's word over your life and start rebuilding those walls!

A DECLARATION OF FAITH for you (based on Isaiah 30):

> Although You have given me the bread of adversity and the water of affliction, my teachers are hidden no more. I am seeing Your wisdom, God, with my own eyes. Whether I turn to the right or the left, I hear Your voice saying, "This is the way, walk in it".
>
> God, You long to be gracious to me. You are rising up and showing me compassion, for You are a God of justice! I am blessed because I seek Your help.
>
> I speak abundance over my financial life. I speak overflow into being. I thank You God for your provision for me and I call this into being.

DO NOT LIVE LIKE THOSE IN THE WORLD

The world today is all about materialism. Bigger houses, flashier cars, electronic devices, overseas trips... it is all about looking GOOD. The advent of credit cards was one of Satan's best ideas. Fooling themselves that they deserve it, people buy things on credit cards or take loans—but when they get them, there is no sense of accomplishment. Instead they feel empty and somehow unhappy because their possessions do not give them meaning.

Previous generations—and only as far back as your grandparents—didn't buy things that they couldn't pay for. They saved for what they wanted. They worked hard, they set their goals, they dreamed about things and they achieved them. When they got what they dreamed about and worked for, they were thankful and their hearts were glad. They had a sense of achievement.

"Then he [Jesus] said to them, 'Watch out!
Be on your guard against all kinds of greed; life
does not consist in an abundance of possessions.'"

Luke 12:15

In today's terms, this is the message I believe God has for us on this issue:

I need My people to come back to the truth. If you can't afford it, you SAVE for it. You cut out the picture of it and you pin it up on your noticeboard in your kitchen, or on your bathroom mirror. You work extra hours, you go without short-term pleasures, and you save until you can buy it. You will then treasure it.

If you buy your first house and take a mortgage, you don't buy the biggest, flashiest house with the three-car garage and the swimming pool! You buy a little house which you can love, turn into a home and make it better for the next person who will live there. You pay off the mortgage as fast as you can, and THEN you buy a flashier house—if this is what you want.

So many of My children seem to think that they must live in luxurious houses, while others think that they don't deserve to. There is no right or wrong here. Different people have different needs and desires—you know this yourself. You know what drives you—what spins your wheels. Some people really care about their surroundings, others don't.

The key here is:

Don't buy things that you can't afford.

If it is important to you, make it happen.

"Suppose one of you wants to build a tower.
Won't you first sit down and estimate the cost to see if you have enough money to complete it? For if you lay the foundation and are not able to finish it, everyone who sees it will ridicule you, saying, 'This person began to build and wasn't able to finish.'"
Luke 14:28-30

If you need to have people around you believe that you are better than you really are, you need to look long and hard at that. Who are you trying to prove yourself to? Your mum or dad? That teacher who said that you would never amount to much? Where is your identity and your worth? Because it certainly is not in Me, even though you may say that I am your God.

A lot of things in life are about self-discipline or self-control. It is one of the fruits of the Spirit. It is about the need to control your impulses and your behaviour so that you can live a good life. There are screeds and screeds of verses in the Bible about the need to have self-control. How else are you going to stop yourself from sinning? How are you going to stop yourself from self-destructing? How are you going to lead a fruitful life?

Everyone has a weakness, an Achilles heel, which makes them vulnerable to sinning. Satan watches and he knows where your weaknesses are. That is how he gets control of people and takes them out of the marching army. He whispers to them to sin—to covet or to lust after something that they WANT which is bad for them—and he takes them down.

Easy credit and high interest loans are two of his most effective weapons.

DO NOT LIVE AS THE WORLD LIVES.

Respect your money. Do not waste it, and do not borrow more than you have. Do not buy things that you want but cannot afford because they WILL be bad for you.

Cash management

There are two basic ways to get ahead financially. One is to spend less and the other is to earn more. Because the latter is harder to achieve for most people, the most obvious way is to spend less.

Often it is not actually a case of spending less, but spending more consciously.

In my financial planning business, a lot of my clients initially have no idea where their income is actually going. I ask them to estimate what they are spending on food, electricity, entertainment, takeaways and so on. We then get three months of their most recent working bank account statements and their credit card statements and we analyse them. Finally, we group their spending and tell them what they are actually spending on these things, and also how often they are buying them. More often than not, it is a real shock to people.

First, work out where your money is going.

You can't change what you aren't aware of. Sit down with your last three months of bank and credit card statements and start grouping your expenditure into categories. These could include:

- Church tithing
- Supermarket and dairies
- Power
- Phone
- Rent/mortgage
- Insurances
- Takeaways
- Coffee/lunches
- Evening meals at restaurants

- Other debt repayment

- Clothing

- Hair/beauty

- Hardware/automotive

- Entertainment (inc. SKY TV and magazines)

- Children's school and sports fees.

Each person will have other categories which are specifically relevant to them, like financially supporting children studying away from home, professional memberships and the like. Just make your own list.

The other thing that you need to keep a record of is how OFTEN you are paying for these things. This is another key number.

When you have done this, you need to sit with it, look at it and ask yourself,

"Is this the best use of my money?"

Pray and ask God for wisdom in reviewing this list. There will be some totals on it which will make you feel uncomfortable. See that feeling as a trigger to make some changes in those areas.

Then act and make changes where you can.

Often, the change lies in being more intentional rather than giving up things.

Things you *may* be able to change:

1. <u>If you are going to the supermarket three to four times a week, work to reduce it to once a week.</u>

Supermarkets are laid out in a certain manner to encourage you to spend more. If you don't believe me, Google "the psychology of supermarket layouts". There are very few people who can pop into the supermarket for one or two things, and not leave with a bag of groceries and a $60 till receipt in their hand! If you are one of those people who can stick to buying two things every time, high five! Join the small club.

I tell my clients to go to the supermarket once a week. It is helpful to go at the same time every week. I used to go at 8:30pm on a Friday night when the supermarket was quiet and I could get in and out without having to experience trolley rage.

There are a lot of people who can go into a dairy for milk and just come out with milk because they believe that dairies are expensive. If you are one of them, and you are also cutting back on your shopping trips, you can use a dairy visit as a backup if you run out of bread, milk or toilet paper during the week. Even if you do sneak in a $2 lolly mix that is sitting right in front of you on the counter as you go to pay, it will still be cheaper than going to the supermarket and emerging with the $60 bag of groceries!

Another thing: milk is often cheaper at the dairy than the supermarket anyway. If you have a family that drinks a lot of milk, scout out a dairy that offers a discount for buying more than one bottle of milk at a time.

If you run short of non-essential food during the week,

tell the people who live with you to take a chill pill. It amuses me no end that my kids can fling open the larder door and dramatically declare that we have no food when the larder looks well stocked with things that apparently are not regarded as food when you are a teenager.

Go figure!

2. <u>Look at your entertainment / coffee / takeaways / treats budget</u>.

I am not suggesting for one moment that you need to stop spending on things which make you happy or keep you sane on a busy day. However I am going to suggest that you review HOW you are spending on these things.

The Journal of Experimental Psychology published an absolutely brilliant study in 2008 by Priya Raghubir and Joydeep Srivastava[1]. They referred to the "pain" of spending using cash, as opposed to spending on a credit card. One of the key findings of their study was that people were prepared to spend less cash on something (in their case, the budget for a Thanksgiving dinner) than they were prepared to spend on a credit card for the same thing.

Their study found that people would spend $145 in cash for dinner but would spend $175 on a credit card for the same dinner. The researchers reasoned that credit card spending was easier for people because the actual payment was in the future (they weren't paying for it now) and because a credit card bill masks what the spending is for (as it contains many transactions).

One of their other findings was that people tended to purchase less healthy things on their credit card than when paying cash for them!

---

1 Raghubir, P., & Srivastava, J. (2008). Monopoly money: The effect of payment coupling and form on spending behavior. Journal of Experimental Psychology: Applied, Volume 14, Issue 3, pages 213–225. https://doi.org/10.1037/1076-898X.14.3.213

In 2016, Anvi Shah and colleagues published a study[2] in the *Journal of Consumer Research* that found that people have more emotional connection with things that they pay cash for, as opposed to using plastic to purchase.

Studies refer to the "psychological pain" of using cash or cheques because the payment is immediate and it is also physical. You are handing over your money for an item or for a service, and a pain receptor in your brain triggers—OUCH! This is costing me something. You do not get the same physiological response with a credit card. At least, until the bill arrives. But by then, it is too late!

Where I am going with this is that you need to start giving yourself cash pocket money. Yes—cash out of the eftpos machine, every payday. This is what you will use for your coffees, your café lunches, your magazines, your impulse buys, your frequent trips to automotive shops to buy car parts that seem to breed in your garage...

There are two advantages to this. The first is that it will psychologically hurt to spend and you will value the item more when you buy it. The second is that once the money is gone, it's gone. Warning: if you have kids, you do need to protect your pocket money from mufti day donations, school trip fees, lost bus cards, wheedling to buy lunches and so on. You can easily find that you have no pocket money and that all of the joy has been sucked out of your life (aka no coffees that week).

3. <u>**Look at your fixed costs spending**</u>.

I recommend **WhatsMyNumber**—
(www.powerswitch.org.nz/whatsmynumber)
to clients who want to review their power and gas spending.

---

2   Shah, A.M., Eisenkraft, N., Bettman, J.R and Chartrand, T.L. (2016). "Paper or Plastic?": How We Pay Influences Post-Transaction Connection. Journal of Consumer Research, Volume 42, Issue 5, Pages 688–708. https://doi.org/10.1093/jcr/ucv056

I personally have saved a lot of money through this platform. WhatsMyNumber was launched in 2011 and is a joint venture between the Electricity Authority and Consumer NZ to encourage New Zealanders to review their power costs and to provide information about switching. This now includes gas as well.

I admit to being very sceptical about making our first switch and I also admit to being slightly flabbergasted by the power savings that we made straight away—without changing anything about how we were using our electricity. The newer generation retailers who sell you power based on spot prices encourage you to change your behaviour and this can save you even more money. You can also shop around for internet and phone pricing as well.

I would be slightly more careful about looking at your insurances. House, car and contents insurances (fire and general insurance) are often cheaper if you go directly to the insurance company rather than through a bank or a broker. However, all of the broker policy wordings and a few of the bank wordings provide better insurance coverage than what you can buy directly from an insurer.

This is especially important if you have individual items with a high value such as jewellery, electronics and sports equipment. Many insurance policies will only cover an item of value up to $1,000, and anything worth more than that must be specified (specifically mentioned separately on the policy schedule), which sometimes also requires you to obtain a valuation.

Brokers will also help you at claim time. If you are time poor, this can also be a real blessing. The same applies when reviewing your personal insurances (life, income protection, medical insurance, etc).

More on this later.

How can you set up a workable budget?

To be fair, this depends entirely on how you think about money.

There are free budgeting tools all over the Internet—for instance, there are some great ones on www.sorted.org.nz. You can buy software packages to use and some of the banks offer packages to their customers. You can run your budget on an Excel spreadsheet. I run mine in a 3B1 notebook (yes, the paper kind). Just find a tool that makes sense to you.

How can I manage my money?

Everyone is different. I have some super smart clients who run their budgets on Excel spreadsheets that give even me a headache (and I quite like spreadsheets). Other clients use online programmes on their phones. Some clients use school maths books (with the quad ruling). It is about finding a method which works for you, doing it every payday, and reviewing it at least every six months.

The key is to create a system that is as simple, as logical and as automated as possible.

A lot of people use the same system as I do to run their cash management (with variations) and it seems to work well for them.

My husband Gary and I get paid fortnightly, but on alternate fortnights. Our pay comes into a working account, which is our main bank account. We have two other bank accounts. One is called the "small payments account" and (you guessed it) the other is the "large payments account". Each payday, money from the main working account is automatically transferred into these two sub-accounts.

The "small payments account" is where we put money for our

monthly bills, like our power, kids' education savings, Gary's SKY TV, our donations to charity and a contribution to an old (but good) superannuation investment which is made monthly.

In this way I never have to worry about having enough money in the working account to cover any direct debits which are coming out on days that don't match with our paydays.

I don't have to check every day that there is enough in the working account and juggle money around... it is all taken care of.

If you have rent that doesn't come out on payday, you may want to add it in here. You may also want to put your mortgage payments into this account if you can't put them straight into a floating mortgage to cover the instalments.

The "large payments account" covers our rates, our fire and general insurance (which is 5% cheaper if you can pay it annually), our regional council rates, our water rates (billed every six months) and our annual life insurance. The latter is a horrendous bill which requires a quiet place, some deep breathing and lavender oil under the nose before the bill is opened, but once again, it is 5% cheaper to pay it annually.

We put our food on a credit card (to get the points, which I use to buy Christmas gifts). Each payday I pay an amount onto that credit card so that the bill is actually covered when it arrives in the mail each month. (Remember, I shop once a week and I have a pretty good handle on the amount I spend each time.)

We also put money away each payday for emergencies and long-term savings, which are two separate accounts that pay higher interest rates. This also goes out straight away by automatic payment.

**After we have withdrawn our
pocket money in cash, the rest
is left for play and the kids!
Remember the magic rule...
once it's gone, it's gone.**

Doing the budget each payday takes me less than five minutes, and it is all recorded in my handy, dandy notebook. The notebook works for me because it is tangible (i.e. not on a computer) and I can check back to see if I have paid a bill because it will be written in the notebook. I also put any bills that need to be paid into the book as they arrive and I even get really clever by putting them in the page that has the pay date that coincides with the due date of the bill. I know... too smart!

You can also set up separate bank accounts for saving for holidays, start-of-year school expenses, Christmas gifts and other things which matter. I have a client who has a savings account for buying hunting equipment as this is really important to him, and another client who saves for high-quality clothes and shoes. (Yes, she always looks amazing!)

It is good to use "bucket thinking" because buckets put clearly defined boundaries around money. If you get the opportunity to attend a CAP money programme, this is what they teach.

Obviously you need to avoid dipping in and out of your buckets and transferring money around. That defeats the entire purpose and could be a sign that your cash management plan has a fatal flaw somewhere. You have either forgotten about or seriously underestimated the cost of some items, or you are not sticking to the guidelines that you have put in place. Go back, work out where the problem is, adjust it and start again. I often talk about leakage—money sneaking out of a hole in a bucket somewhere. Find your leak and plug it!

<u>What about emergencies?</u>

Everyone needs to have a rainy day account, because

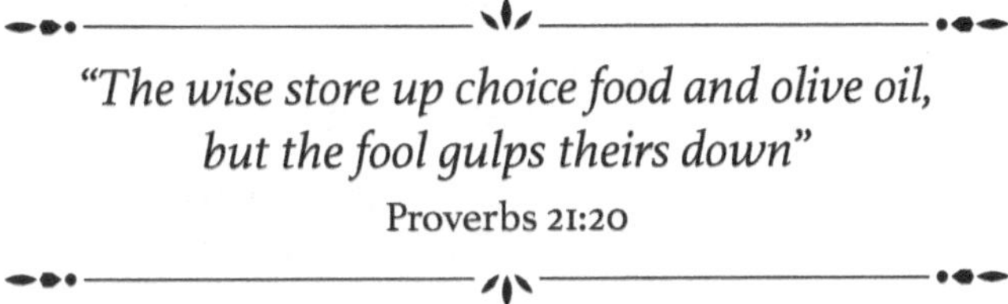

"The wise store up choice food and olive oil,
but the fool gulps theirs down"
Proverbs 21:20

This account is to be set aside for EMERGENCIES. Not the Boxing Day sales, not concert tickets, not the cheap airfares that suddenly appeared on your Facebook feed... but Real Emergencies. Things like hot water cylinders blowing up, the warning light coming on in the car, the cat getting in a fight and needing to go to the vet. Losing your job and needing to pay the bills until you get a new one. Getting cancer and having to be off work for a while for treatment. Real, raw emergencies.

Conventional financial planning wisdom is that you need to have at least three months of household income (three months of pay) that you can access in an emergency. It is good wisdom because a three month stand-down on income protection or mortgage protection insurance makes the premiums a lot cheaper than a four or eight-week stand-down. However, anything is better than nothing—and to be honest, most people have next to nothing.

You can have your emergency savings in a bank savings account or in a redraw facility on your mortgage. The latter will save you the cost of interest.

I advise the "worst offenders" to have their emergency savings in a completely separate bank to their day-to-day bank. They cannot see the money on their internet banking, it cannot be electronically transferred to their working account, and they physically have to go to a bank during working hours to get the money out. That generally slows people down long enough to evaluate if the situation is actually an emergency or just a really strong want.

Work out (from your cash management plan) how much you can save to get your emergency account underway. As I say, anything is better than nothing. Even $10 a week to start with is something!

And remember, if you do take money from the emergency account, put it back. There will be another emergency in your future somewhere, trust me on that!

A side hustle.

If you have the time, you can always pick up some additional income through an extra job. I have clients who have a separate weekend job, who have small home based businesses, or who are being UBER drivers. Once again, the key with this is to ensure that the time that you are giving up is offset by the additional income being used wisely.

One last point...

If you are participating in dishonest dealings, you cannot be honoured.

Proverbs 20:23 tells us that,

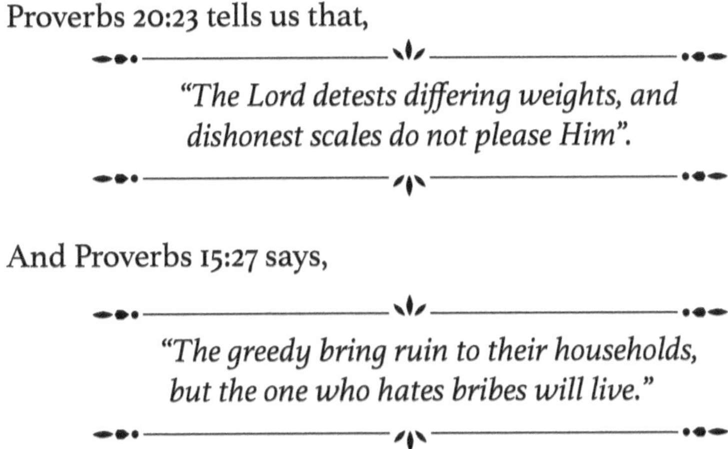

*"The Lord detests differing weights, and
dishonest scales do not please Him".*

And Proverbs 15:27 says,

*"The greedy bring ruin to their households,
but the one who hates bribes will live."*

If you are ripping people off by not paying them fairly for their work, if you are taking cash under the table, if you are cheating the system... you are not bringing heaven on earth. It is not how things are done in the Kingdom.

If you dishonour, you cannot be honoured.

Look at 1 Timothy 6, especially verses 3–10. Bring this before God, and ask Him if there are any areas of your life that you need to repent for, and behaviours that you need to change.

SUMMARY

- Create a spending plan—and try to stick to it.
- Review where your money is currently being spent and see if you are happy with your current spending patterns.
- Create an emergency bank account and aim for 3 months of income in it.

	Money OUT	Money IN
Wages		$
NEEDS		
Tithing		
Rent/mortgage		
Food		
Power/gas		
Phone		
Transport		
Insurance		
School/childcare		
SAVINGS		
Emergency fund		
Other savings		
WANTS		
Pocket money		
Movies		
Takeaways		
SURPLUS		
THIS NUMBER SHOULD BALANCE	$	$

DEAL WITH YOUR DEBT

The Holy Spirit said that debt is about giving the control over your life to someone else. It is like selling your soul to the devil.

When you owe someone money, you are ceding your personal authority to them, because they now have a lien over your life. It may be a bank, a money lender, a family member or a friend, but you have surrendered control to them. This is why people hate debt. They are happy enough to get into it, but then they hate it in their hearts. Why? Because their soul man knows that they have sold part of their soul to someone else.

"The rich rule over the poor and the borrower
is a slave to the lender."

Proverbs 22:7

Debt is not good. It destroys marriages, it breaks up families and it causes so many mental health issues. Most people with depression and anxiety owe money. They have credit card debt, they owe money in fines, they owe money everywhere, and it damages their brains. Their spirits feel the bondage that they have entered into more strongly than others.

It is never my desire that anyone gets into debt for ANYTHING, the Lord says.

**If you feel that I have called you
on a mission trip but you have to
borrow the money to go—trust Me,
I did not tell you to do that!**

I would never have told you to borrow money to go—that is a LIE. I wanted you to learn how to SAVE, to learn how to dream and how to plan to achieve goals. Please do not go to Bible College on a loan. Please work really hard and save the money to go. What is the point of going to Bible College to come out IN BONDAGE? You won't be able to break anything in Satan's kingdom when you are in bondage yourself.

If you have got yourself into debt, you have a moral obligation to repay the money that you have taken. God's Word reminds us,

*"The wicked borrow and do not repay, but the
righteous give generously."*

Psalm 37:21

*"Do not be deceived; God cannot be mocked.
A man reaps what he sows. The one who sows to
please his sinful nature will reap destruction; the one
who sows to please the spirit, from the spirit will
reap eternal life."*

Galatians 6:7

I am a fair and just God. I demand honest weights on scales (Proverbs 20:23) and I pay an honest day's wages for an honest day's work. You reap what you sow and you harvest what you plant. Do not ask me to supernaturally remove your debt, because I cannot. It goes against everything that I believe in and everything which I stand for as God. Encouraging My children to pray for their debt to be forgiven is not a biblical precept, and do not do this for others. It is a LIE from the King of Lies. Would you pray to ask Me to help you to murder your spouse, or to help you to rob a store? When your debt is not forgiven or taken away, you will then believe that I do not care, or that I do not hear your prayers and then Satan has won. If I were to get your debt forgiven, I would have ROBBED the person or the organisation which lent you the money. I am not a God who steals.

I will however help you in any way that I can to get rid of your debt. When you step out and start to walk away from the path of bondage, the angels will sing and dance around you, and I will help you. You will see My hand on your life and I promise that I will uphold you. Satan will not like it as you throw off the shackles, but I will be with you and protect you all the way.

*"Although the Lord gives you the bread of
adversity and the water of affliction, your
teachers will be hidden no more; with your own
eyes you will see them. Whether you turn to the
right or to the left, your ears will hear a voice
behind you saying,
'This is the way; walk in it.'"*

Isaiah 30:20-21

<u>Debt management</u>

Controlling your debt is a key to having a powerful life.

Debt is the one area that can really wipe people out—financially, emotionally, mentally and spiritually. Having debt go bad can affect your credit rating for years, which makes it hard to get money in the future and to access utilities like power and phone accounts. It can also result in a poor allocation of your financial resources. If you are paying all of your surplus income towards a debt for something from the past, you are not sowing into your future.

Debt causes worry and stress, which can lead to physical and mental health issues. It's a well-known fact that money worries are a leading cause of relationship breakdown. Worry and stress also open the door to FEAR, which is the opposite of faith. Fear can shift your focus from God onto temporal things and put you into survival mode instead of revival mode.

Simplistically, there are two types of debt: the debt you take on to finance assets which increase in value, and the debt you take on to finance lifestyle and things which decrease in value.

Managing "good" debt finance.

"Good" debt finance would include things like a mortgage on your first home, a loan to buy a business which you can grow, and arguably (following on from God's words!) student loans which can enable you to get a qualification that will eventually give you access to a high-paying job or trade.

The key with a mortgage
or a student loan is to develop a
strategy to pay it off as quickly
as you can.

With mortgages, you can choose between FLOATING rates and FIXED rates. At present, fixed rates are much lower than floating rates, so they are more attractive. However, a fixed rate is a contract and if you break that contract, there is a penalty to be paid. If you decide that you can pay off an additional $400 a month and you then fix your loan for two years on that assumption, you are contractually obliged to pay the additional $400 a month for the term of the fixed rate. If you lose your job, or if you get sick and suddenly you can't make the additional $400 a month, you are deemed to have broken your mortgage contract and the bank can ping you with a financial penalty if you try to revert back to making the minimum payment. Some banks do allow you to change the payments during the term of the contract, so check with your bank if this is the case. (My bank allows you to increase but not decrease your payments.)

This is where floating loans come into play! If you were to float an amount equivalent to $400 a month for one year and fix the rest of the lending for one year, you can put your $400 a month into the floating loan but you are not obliged to make the payment. If life throws you a curve ball, you can revert back to paying only the interest on the floating amount and then pick things up again when you have spare cash. Yes, you will pay a slightly higher interest rate, but treat the higher costs as insurance. The actual dollar amount will be small, and you have a "Plan B" strategy.

The next step in creating a debt reduction strategy is to have your floating loan in a revolving credit or redraw facility. This is like a mortgage overdraft, but you only pay interest on the amount that is in debit. If you have a redraw facility (or mortgage overdraft) of $20,000 but you only have $4,800 in debit, you only pay interest on the $4,800—not the $20,000. When you have paid off the $4,800, you can choose to transfer over another amount from your fixed-rate loan, and put the revolving credit facility/ mortgage overdraft back into a debit amount before you refix it, and then pay this off again.

This is what we are trying to achieve:

Year 1—mortgage of $300,000
Float $4,800 to repay in full ($400 a month)
and fix $295,200

Year 2—mortgage of $295,200
Float $4,800 to repay in full and fix $290,400

Year 3—mortgage of $290,400
Float $4,800 to repay in full and fix $285,600

Year 4—mortgage of $285,600
Float $4,800 to repay in full and fix $280,800

Year 5—mortgage of $280,800
Float $4,800 to repay in full and fix $276,000

Get the idea?

Of course the actual amounts of the mortgage will be LESS than the above figures. It will depend on the term of the mortgage and the interest rate. If you go to www.sorted.org.nz and look under the tools tab, they have some really good mortgage calculators that you can play with to get more accurate figures.

To give you an idea of how the strategy would work with real numbers, let's assume we get a mortgage of $300,000 at a 6% interest rate with a term of 20 years. The minimum repayments for this are $2,149 a month, and the total amount that you will pay over 20 years is $515,472. So, $300,000 is the original amount that you borrowed and $215,472 is interest over 20 years of mortgage. In other words, the amount of interest you will pay is 71% of the amount that you originally borrowed.

If you were to pay an additional $400 a month towards this mortgage, it will take roughly five years off the term of the mortgage—so it will be fully repaid in 15 years instead of 20. The total repayments that you make will come to $453,842 because the interest will be only $153,842—that's 51% of the amount that you originally borrowed.

This is an interest saving of $61,630, which is a lot of money by anyone's account!

An even better benefit is that you now have an additional five years of your working life with no debt.

Depending on how you are tracking, you can save five years of your mortgage payments ($152,940 in total) to add to your retirement savings, or you can save up and use this money for a trip, a new car, to help your kids, to help your church… you have choices!

It is a very cost-effective strategy to keep your emergency savings stashed in your redraw facility, instead of having it in a bank account earning very little. That way you save yourself the floating mortgage rate in debit interest! You can access the money at any time by doing an internet banking transfer out of the redraw and into your working account—just as you would do if you had the money in your emergency savings account.

A lot of banks and some mortgage brokers say that you should put your wages into your redraw facility and then live out of it. Unless you are fully prepared to track your money coming in and money going out of your redraw every day, I strongly advise you not to do this. You have to be spending less than you put in to get any benefit from this strategy. The reality is that the majority of people do not track their money like this, and therefore are going backwards each month, racking up more debt.

I am a financial adviser with an adorable husband who has a very different money management strategy to mine. That said, we have never 'lived out of' our redraw facility account. We have paid our monthly surplus payments into our redraw each month but no money comes back out of that redraw, under threat of imminent death. It is a black hole—whatever goes in there STAYS in there. It has been a much easier way to track that we are gaining ground. If there was no money in the cheque account, there was NO MONEY. It meant that we did without until payday or raided a back-up account which was then replaced.

We have sometimes borrowed money out of the redraw for things, but always paid it back over and above the normal payments. Once, I got so grumpy with my husband that I even charged him interest on what he 'borrowed' from the redraw facility to buy another new car. He went to work and told all his mates. I wasn't sure how I felt about how that made me look, but I still charged him interest. It did have the result of making him much less likely to ask for a loan from the redraw facility, so I guess that it wasn't all bad!

Be very aware of the TERM of your loan. People seldom live in one house for their whole lives. You buy your first house, and the bank gives you a mortgage with a term of up to 30 years. Five years later, you are buying a house with a garden for the swing set, because there is a baby on the way. You get a new mortgage with a 30-year term. Ten years later, you are buying a house with more bedrooms and you get a mortgage with a 30-year term. Eight years later, you are buying your "dream home" with the lovely outdoor area and a second lounge, and you get a mortgage with another 30-year term. You are in your late forties or early fifties and you have a mortgage with a 30-year term! If you make the minimum mortgage payments (as a lot of people do), you will still have a mortgage in your 70s.

You would be astonished by the number of people I meet who have no idea that their mortgage term is going to run well past their predicted retire-from-work date.

When you hit your forties, please
make sure that any mortgage you
have is going to be cleared before
you plan to retire.

If you are buying a new home with a mortgage, please ensure that the mortgage term will end ideally two to five years before you plan to retire.

STUDENT LOANS are an interesting phenomenon. At present, if you stay in New Zealand after you graduate from University, your student loan will remain interest-free when you start working. You are simply required by Inland Revenue to make a minimum payment of 12% of your income over $20,020.

People ask if they should repay their student loans. If you are planning to leave New Zealand and travel overseas for longer than 183 days, you definitely should. If you leave the country to travel for more than six months, you will be charged interest on the loan, and you have the issue of having to send money back from overseas to meet the minimum payments (which are based on the size of your loan). When you come back and have been based here for 183 days, you can apply for the loan to become interest-free again.

When you apply for a mortgage, the bank will take your student loan repayment requirements into account when working out how much debt you will be able to service. A high student loan balance means that you will be able to borrow less for your house. On that basis, you may wish to pay off your student loan faster OR accumulate the money that you were planning to put on the loan in an investment of some kind which you can access when you want to buy your house.

Managing "bad" finance.

"Bad" finance covers a wide range of things, like credit card debt, finance card debt, high-interest (unsecured) personal loans, and payday lending. It can also cover things like car loans—although sometimes a car is a necessity if it enables you to hold down a job.

"Bad" finance includes buying things like furniture and whiteware, as they decrease in value. Again, these things are sometimes a necessity. This is where looking out for interest-free deals can become really useful. Do your very best to pay it off within the interest-free time frame, because the interest rates for these loans after this can be eye watering. That's the catch!

Make it a rule never to take finance for a depreciating asset (one that drops in value) for a term which is longer than the time you will have the asset. For instance, if you borrow money against your house to buy a car, make the term of the car mortgage no more than five years. If you were to take a car loan from a finance company, the term of that loan would be between three and five years. You will be trading the car again within that time, so why would you take a 20-year loan for something that you will not own in three to five years' time? Borrowing the money against your house will make the interest rate lower (unless the car dealer has a special interest rate going), but if you take a loan over 20 years, it is entirely self-defeating. The same principle applies when adding to your mortgage to buy furniture and whiteware.

With regard to the other high-interest debts, there is no easy fix at all... no magic wand.

Creating a debt reduction plan.

The first thing that you need to do is to make a LIST of all your debt. You need to know the amount that you owe, what the interest rate of the loan is, and what the minimum repayments are. If you have started a cash management plan, I hope that you have identified a surplus amount each payday—even if it is just $20. This surplus can be used to reduce your debt.

Then pick off the loans, one at a time. Ideally, you should start with the one that has the highest interest rate. Make only the minimum payments on all the others and put all your extra money into that one high-interest loan. Track the balance of the loan once a month, because you will see that you are making progress.

Once this loan has been paid off, have a small celebration!

Then put the loan payment for this loan and the extra amount that you were paying into wiping out the next loan on your list.

If this seems too overwhelming for you, I would suggest that you start this strategy with your smallest loan, because you will see the "win" much more quickly. Get an accountability partner. Make it someone that you are slightly scared of, and someone who is not afraid to tell it like it is. I have a friend who shouts me a coffee once a month, and we track her financial progress. It is more 'real' if you have to confess to someone each month about how things are tracking. I am a member of a business accountability group and I will work weekends so that I don't have to confess that I have stuffed up with my targets for each month! Accountability is a powerful thing.

You can sometimes get a debt consolidation loan. This can be useful if the interest rate is LESS than you are paying on the multitude of loans that you have, and if the fees are not too high to get it established. This makes it much cleaner. However, the idea is that you keep the payments the same as what you were paying on your previous basket of loans. You are trying to get ahead!

Sometimes banks offer transfers of credit card debt onto a new credit card at zero interest for a fixed time (usually six or 12 months). Watch out for the small print on this. Sometimes you will be required to transfer your accounts to the new bank, or you will be required to close all your other credit cards. Also be aware that any purchases that you make on the new credit card will be charged interest straight away, and any payments that you make onto the card are first applied to clear the interest-free debt (leaving you with the balance to settle with interest).

For example, if you transfer $2,000 onto an "interest-free for six months" credit card, and then use the card to buy your groceries because it was a bad week, the interest will start at 19.95% on those groceries and will be charged at 19.95% until that $2,000 interest-free debt has been cleared. You can't whack the grocery money back on the following week and think that you are back to where you were. This is a trap for young players!

The best way to use this option is to work out how you can clear that debt within the interest-free period ($76.93 a week for $2,000 over six months), and not to put any new debits onto that credit card.

Beware of the lies around debt.

As I said previously, the most effective way for Satan to take someone out like an American football quarterback is to get them into a spiral of debt that they can't find their way out of.

If you start on the debt
reduction journey, do not drink
from the poisoned chalice of
discouragement.

As Rachel Hunter used to earnestly tell us in the Pantene shampoo commercials, "It won't happen overnight, but it will happen". This is where regularly TRACKING the amount that you owe will help you to see that you are making headway. When we had our mortgage, I used to track it monthly and write the latest balance owing on the back of the bank statement. You can then look back and see the tangible progress.

Do not believe the lie that you cannot live without a credit card. People lived without credit cards for thousands of years. They are a relatively new thing. I like the "barefoot investor" idea of having a savings account to replace the things that go onto your credit card and using that instead.

However, in my experience as a financial adviser, getting clients to stop using their credit cards is equivalent to asking people to climb Mount Everest while wearing jandals and carrying a baby elephant—it is an idea that will never happen. In fact, in nearly two decades as a financial adviser, I have more clients who have been to Base Camp at Mount Everest than clients who have gone cold turkey and cancelled their credit cards.

Credit cards are like an addiction, and I mean that in the purest sense of the word.

PLEASE—if you need to—please find the strength to cut them up, and please do not replace them.

The same thing goes for getting a debt consolidation loan and then racking up more debt. There seems to be a psychology around going from ten debts to one debt. It does not mean that you can then get more debt! Remember, debt is about the dollar value you owe and not the number of individual debts! I know that this may seem perfectly logical to some people, but the number of times that I have seen this reverse logic in action is absolutely staggering. This has to be a lie of Satan.

I like the verse in Zechariah 4, verse 10, which says:

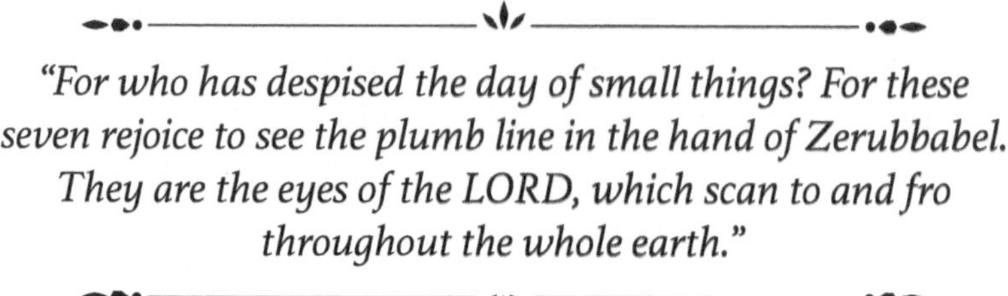

"For who has despised the day of small things? For these seven rejoice to see the plumb line in the hand of Zerubbabel. They are the eyes of the LORD, which scan to and fro throughout the whole earth."

Other versions of the Bible talk about "the day of small beginnings". The decision to start digging yourself out of debt is exactly this—a day of small beginnings. It can look as though it is meaningless because you may not see the fruits of your labour for months or even years. But the Lord REJOICES because He knows that this is the start of something POWERFUL. For some of you, this is the start of shaking off the chains of BONDAGE—mental and emotional bondage which has rendered you powerless and taken you off the path that God had for your life.

A plumb line is a weight suspended on the end of a string. It hangs straight down and gives a builder an exact and perfect vertical line to use when creating a frame for a structure. God talks a lot in the Bible about being a builder—about laying cornerstones (building foundations), building houses on rocks and sand, building temples, having holy upper rooms, and dwelling (living) in houses of righteousness.

Having a plumb line is an indication of "true north". It is a straight and perfect line. There is no better line to be had in all of the earth. It is the best standard. There are other places in the Bible which mention a plumb line and it has been interpreted as righteousness. Righteousness is about doing what is right—about having ethical behaviour, about following God's precepts.

In the book of Ezra, Zerubbabel was the governor of Judah. History has recorded that he laid the foundation for the Temple. He was given sanction to rebuild the Temple and return the sacred Temple vessels that Nebuchadnezzar II had preserved after the conquest of Babylon. He was restoring the holy place of the Lord.

It's not that big a leap to say that you are restoring the holy place of the Lord if you are taking back the control and authority of your debt and your financial situation.

'God, please cancel my debt'.

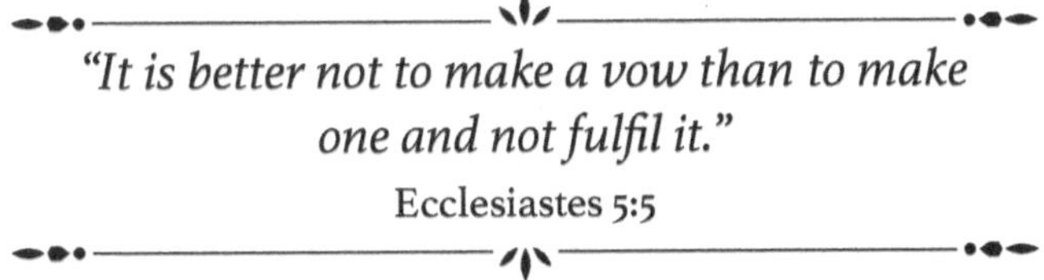

"It is better not to make a vow than to make one and not fulfil it."

Ecclesiastes 5:5

It distresses me greatly when I go onto Facebook pages of well-known preachers and see literally hundreds of people posting that they are in financial trouble and want prayer for it. It also distresses me to hear people asking for prayer to have their debt miraculously cancelled.

As the Holy Spirit began this chapter by saying, that's usually not how it rolls, because it goes against His very nature. Yes, God can perform miracles, but He is also a fair and just God. If you have borrowed money from a business and God makes it so that you don't have to pay the money back, you are robbing that business. You are financially disadvantaging the owners or the shareholders of that business. That asset, which they lent to you, is lost to them.

Please don't ask God to do things which go against His very nature.

Yes, He owns the cattle on a thousand hills, but He did not get them by stealing them from the farmer next door.

You have to pay your way out, just as you borrowed your way in... but God will honour your stewardship of your finances.

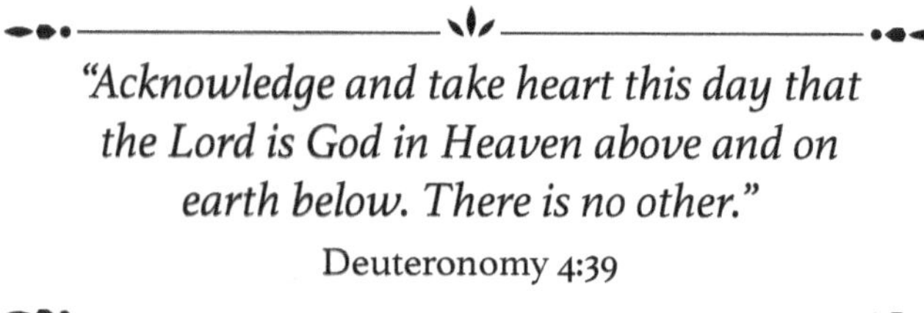

"Acknowledge and take heart this day that the Lord is God in Heaven above and on earth below. There is no other."

Deuteronomy 4:39

SUMMARY

- Make a list of your debts—the amounts, the interest rates and the terms of the loans.

- Look at your cash management surplus and see if it makes sense to use all of it or some of it for debt reduction.

- Start tracking the amount of your debt on a regular basis (monthly).

- Repay the highest interest debt first.

- Review your use of credit cards to see if you need to change your current strategy.

Debt repayment schedule.

	Amount	Interest rate (highest to lowest)	Minimum payment	Additional amount to add to debt repayment
Debt 1: Start here				
Debt 2				
Debt 3				

KEY 2

HAVING WEALTH
IS NOT EVIL

I cannot believe how My children have let Satan corrupt one of My blessings to them. If you cannot have wealth and if you cannot STORE wealth, how can I make sure that there is enough money to get My projects done on this earth? I have to pass money around the world in an orderly and structured fashion. I need to give it to My children, and KNOW that they are going to be good stewards of what I give them, until I need them to pass it on.

People are literally dying out there because My own children are living under the lie that poverty is more godly than wealth. Jesus was the role model for how a godly life should be lived—He showed My children how to do it. For instance, how do you think He got around with the 12 disciples? While He personally didn't have a lot of money, his brothers and sisters in Me who did have the money made sure that everything He needed to do got funded. It was the same with Paul! The money for their ministries came from fellow believers! If people back then believed that it wasn't godly to have money, the new testament would not exist, would it? Sorry—this lie makes Me really cross.

Paul, writing in 1 Corinthians 16:2, says,

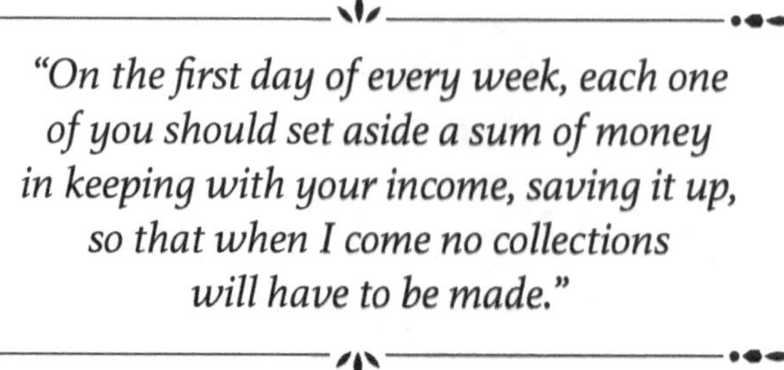

*"On the first day of every week, each one
of you should set aside a sum of money
in keeping with your income, saving it up,
so that when I come no collections
will have to be made."*

There are two issues here. There is wealth, and then there is the use of wealth as a replacement for Me. The latter is not godly. There are people who enjoy a great glass of wine and people who drink to excess, which destroys their lives and those around them. The latter is not godly. There are people who remain sexually chaste, and others who have sex with lots of people because it is what young people do these days. The latter is not godly.

Satan uses THE LOVE OF WEALTH and the perceived sense of power and control that it brings to keep people away from Me. It gives people a really false sense of security.

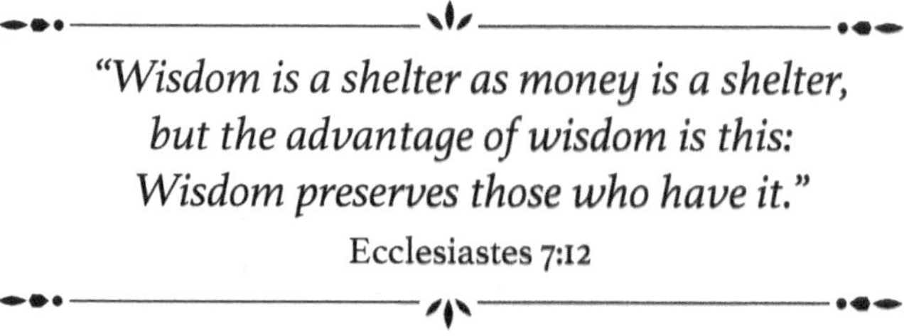

*"Wisdom is a shelter as money is a shelter,
but the advantage of wisdom is this:
Wisdom preserves those who have it."*
Ecclesiastes 7:12

'Self-made' people do not feel that they need a God because they have it all under control. The world worships self-made, financially wealthy people. I don't really understand why. Spiritually, many of them are desolate paupers. They are broken inside and truly lost. These are the people who need Me as much as the people living in the gutter.

Love of an excess of wealth is just as bad as being a homeless street person.

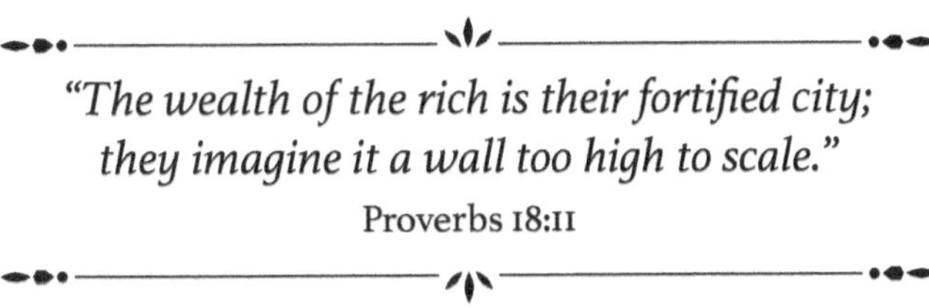

"The wealth of the rich is their fortified city;
they imagine it a wall too high to scale."
Proverbs 18:11

My children need to accept that it is okay to have money, and that you have a responsibility to steward it wisely. You do not squander it on things that wither and blow away, like the latest big screen TV. Rather, you put it in the storehouse. You give some of it to your church and you save the rest. There may come a day that I will ask you to release some of that money for My purpose, but I will let you know. It may just be a little or it may be a lot. If I know that you will use the wealth wisely (note that I did not say YOUR wealth, because it came from Me), I will give you more and more of it.

"Command those who are rich in this
present world not to be arrogant nor to put
their hope in wealth, which is not certain, but
to put their hope in God, who richly provides
us with everything for our enjoyment.
Command them to do good, to be rich in
good deeds, and to be generous and willing
to share. In this way, they will lay up treasure
for themselves in a firm foundation for the
coming age, so that they may take hold of
the life that is truly life."
1 Timothy 6:17-19

I also want to be able to give my children GOOD THINGS. I love you! I want you to be able to have your heart's desires! I want to be able to give you resources which you can use to delight yourselves! I will give you money for everyday things, and then money to use for things which gladden your heart. If one of your children desperately wanted something with all of their heart, wouldn't you work with them to help them to get it? You would give them money towards it, or help them to get a job to pay for it. You would drive them to their job and give what you could to help them to achieve their dream. When they get there, their joy would be your joy! Their achievement would be your achievement! So it is with Me. I delight in your delight. Nothing pleases Satan more than hope deferred, because it makes the heart sick. I want you to have hope achieved! When hope is achieved, your heart grows stronger. You stand taller. You grow, you learn. This is what I want for you.

<u>Retirement planning</u>
(aka achieving financial independence from work)

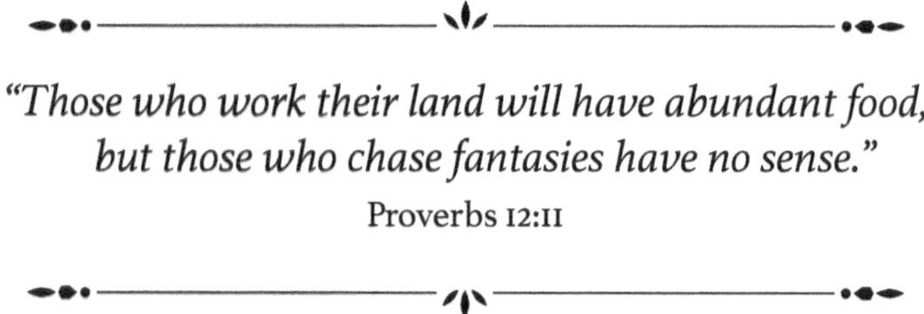

*"Those who work their land will have abundant food,
but those who chase fantasies have no sense."*
Proverbs 12:11

The number of our days is not determined by us but by the Lord. Having said that, we have to plan as if we are going to have a long life, and that will include setting money aside to provide for our retirement.

Retirement in itself is an interesting concept. Retirement didn't exist until the industrial revolution. It was widely introduced in the 1930s because (to be brutally honest) the US government needed to get older people out of the factories in order to get the younger ones in. This was to ease unemployment and to improve productivity in an unbelievably tough workplace. The retirement age was 65, and the average life expectancy was 68! These days, the retirement age is still 65, but your average life expectancy is actually 90. That is a lot of years of sitting around....

At the same time, retirement is starting to look more like what our ancestors had before the 1930s. A lot of people are working part-time when they reach 65 and will keep doing so as long as they have the health, mental capacity and interest to keep going. Sometimes it is for the money, but more often than not, it is for the social aspects of being with other people, for fun, for mental stimulation, or simply to give you a reason to get up and get going in the morning.

Today, we seem to have a mentality that you have to go hard out until you hit a certain age or you hit the wall, and then it's all over.

From a mental perspective, it's not always that healthy to go cold turkey into retirement, especially if you love your work, your clients or your colleagues.

Back in the "pre-retirement" days, people pulled back a bit on their work hours as they aged and paced themselves so that they always had the energy to work—even if it was in small amounts as they got much older. From my observations, clients who do this today seem to adjust a lot better to life as they age.

However, there will come a point where you just don't want to work anymore, and that is the point at which it will be really useful to have some retirement savings.

One of the easiest ways to save for retirement in New Zealand is through KiwiSaver. This was launched in 2007 and was modelled on the Australian and Canadian superannuation schemes. Each person can have their own specific KiwiSaver for their lifetime and can even have the fund manager of their choice if they wish.

Any New Zealander (citizen or resident) can open a KiwiSaver. If you are under the age of 16, your parents or guardians have to sign the application for you.

There is no longer a maximum age for opening a KiwiSaver—this was recently removed.

Your KiwiSaver funds are generally only available to you to access for the purchase of your first home (criteria apply) and when you reach the national age of retirement (currently 65). You can also access your KiwiSaver if you are terminally ill or leaving New Zealand permanently. Provisions are in place for you to access your KiwiSaver in case of hardship, but this can be quite difficult to achieve. All the conditions for accessing your KiwiSaver before the national age of retirement are noted on the IRD website.

If you are a waged earner (where you have PAYE deducted from your income), your employer is required by law to contribute 3% of your gross income to your KiwiSaver (less employer superannuation contributions tax) if you are also personally contributing at least 3% of your gross salary into your KiwiSaver. You can contribute 3%, 4%, 6%, 8% or 10% of your salary, and you can change your contribution rate at any time by filling in a new KS2 form and giving it to your payroll person.

If you are not a waged earner, you are deemed to be self-employed. You can pay in any amount that you want. However, if you are aged between 18 and 65, it is a good idea to contribute at least $1,042.86 a year ($87 a month) so that you qualify for the full Government tax credit amount of $521.43 per annum.

The Government-paid member tax credit is calculated on your personal contributions for the year from 1 July to 30 June. For every dollar that you contribute up to $1,042.86, the Government will put in 50 cents as a member credit.

I have clients who are not working and I encourage them to try to put in their $87 a month as there is no investment in NZ which guarantees them a 50% return on their 12 months contributions!

People who are on benefits (including ACC or income protection claims) can put in a monthly amount by direct debit like self-employed people do. If you are over the age of 65, you no longer get the member tax credits, but your KiwiSaver is on call as an investment for you.

I have never met a person who complained of having too much money when they retired. Most people worry that they don't have enough, and unfortunately some of them are correct. National Superannuation is adjusted for increases in the cost of living across the board, BUT the items that always increase more than the cost of living each year (electricity, rates and insurance) are the main costs of retirees.

It is hard to be a home owner in retirement, but it is worse if you are trying to rent.

Rental cost increases can be crippling—plus it can be traumatic to find new accommodation if your landlord sells your home.

The thing with saving for retirement is to start early.

There is a fairly blunt instrument known as the Rule of 72. How it works for investment calculations is that you divide 72 by the rate of return on an investment, and that tells you how long it will take to double the investment.

When you are saving for retirement, doubles matter. For example, if you are 30 years old and you start saving into a KiwiSaver with a balanced asset allocation which may have an annual average return of 5%, it will take 14.4 years to double your money. You therefore have two 'doubles' before you reach the age of 65. If you are starting out at 35 and want your two doubles, you will need to invest more aggressively to get a higher rate of return. If you go for a growth fund with an average annual return of 7%, it will take 10.28 years to double your money, so you will still get your two doubles in before the age of 65. However, if you are 25 and invest into a growth fund (because you are not going to use your KiwiSaver for a house deposit) you will get THREE doubles.

Albert Einstein is reputed to have said, "Compound interest is the eighth wonder of the world. He who understands it, earns it; he who doesn't, pays it."

The potential investment time horizon matters when you are setting your investment asset allocation. If you are planning on using your KiwiSaver (or an investment) in less than two years, go for cash or a conservative asset allocation. The reason for this is that you want some certainty around the balance of the investment when you need it. If your investment is 50% shares (a balanced asset allocation) and the share markets drop by 35% (as they did over six weeks when Covid-19 hit the western world), you are slightly screwed if you need that money at that time.

The same works in reverse. If you are young, have your KiwiSaver in a conservative asset allocation, and won't be using it for a home deposit, why? You can't get the money until you are in your 60s, so you may as well ramp it up a bit. Working on the previous example of the Rule of 72, a growth fund will get you three doubles if you are 25 now. A conservative fund will barely get you two doubles (if it returns 3.5% per annum).

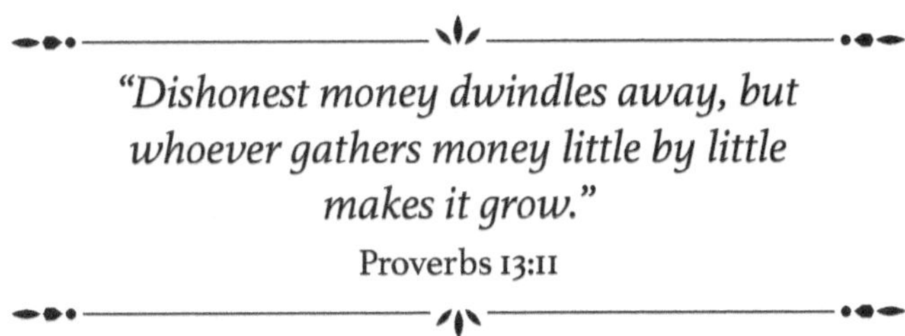

> *"Dishonest money dwindles away, but whoever gathers money little by little makes it grow."*
>
> Proverbs 13:11

There are some good investment risk profile assessments on the Internet. There is a questionnaire on www.sorted.org.nz that will help you to work out what your investment risk profile is. Some of the KiwiSaver funds have a 'life stages' or 'lifetimes' option which is also a good guide to the type of fund you should be in, depending on your age.

How to choose a KiwiSaver.

This isn't as easy as it looks. There is information available on www.sorted.org.nz, but at the time of writing this, it is fairly short-term focused. KiwiSaver is a marathon, not a sprint, so a one-year return comparison is meaningless. If you can get a 10-year return comparison, that is much better—especially now that it also includes a decent market correction.

If ethical investing is important to you, you can go to www.mindfulmoney.nz and have a look at the data on this website. It tells you what your KiwiSaver is invested in but do be aware that the data could be outdated (more than 12 months old).

It is not a good idea to choose your KiwiSaver based solely on the fees; that is like choosing a restaurant based on the colour of the carpet. You go to a restaurant for the FOOD. You take out an investment for the RETURNS, and the more consistent the returns, the better. Compare KiwiSavers on their return after fees and before tax, making sure that the asset allocations are comparable before you compare the returns (so that you are comparing apples with apples). Some balanced funds have a 40% fixed interest component and the rest is growth, while others have 60% fixed interest and a lower growth allocation. Fixed interest is the capital-stable part of your KiwiSaver, but it usually makes lower returns. It is unfair to compare a fund with a 40% fixed interest allocation to a fund with a 60% fixed interest allocation.

Your KiwiSaver (and your other investments) will be very important to your financial future, so pay attention to what is happening with them and review them once a year. You get a statement annually, so this is a good time to have a deep look at it.

I also encourage clients to save for their retirement outside of their KiwiSaver.

KiwiSaver is great, but you can't access the money if you need to help a family member or have to retire before the age of 65 because of poor health. Having long-term savings in a unit trust (which is basically the same underlying investment structure as a KiwiSaver, but without the locked-in feature) is a great option for ensuring that you have access to money if life doesn't go according to plan.

There are many investment options where you can save a small amount each payday and just let it accumulate.

If doing this type of analysis is not
your happy place, PAY someone
to do it for you.

Approach a financial adviser and ask if they recommend more than one KiwiSaver or managed fund investment. (You want someone who has a few arrows in their quiver and not just one. If they only recommend one, guess which one they will recommend for you?)

It is worth spending a few hundred bucks every five years to check that you are on the right track. You should easily gain more than this in investment return, and you also have the peace of mind that you are on the right track.

DO NOT ROB ME

Oxygen, light, your heartbeat...it all comes from me. When you choose to become a follower of Me, one of My children, you come under My guidance and authority. One of the things that I teach is that you must bring your firstfruits to the storehouse.

There are teachings in the Bible about the widow's mite (Mark 12:41-44), and the woman who used the last of what she had to make Elijah's bread. They are there for a REASON. You cannot say, "That was nice for them, but I am in a worse position than they were so I must hang onto my money as if I am drowning and this is a life ring." That is not how it works in My kingdom. You must follow the principles of life. You must step out in faith to see your faith restored. You must hold lightly to hold more.

You must give the firstfruits into the storehouse of your church. If you have a problem with that, you must come and seek Me and My word on this for you.

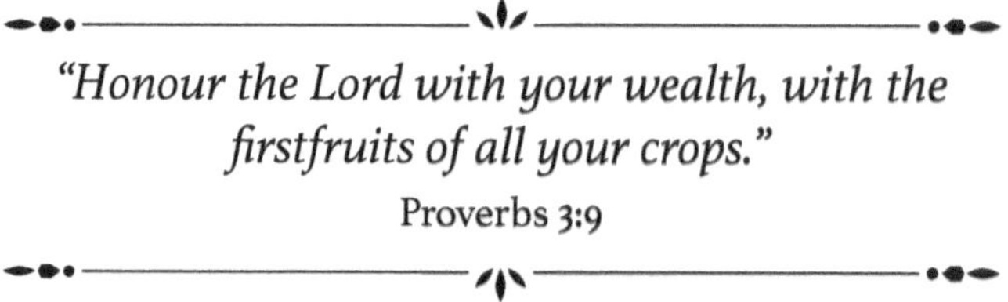

*"'Bring the whole tithe into the storehouse,
that there may be food in my house. Test me in
this,' says the Lord Almighty, 'and see if I will
not throw open the floodgates of Heaven and
pour out so much blessing that there will not
be room enough to store it.'"*
Malachi 3:10

My Word talks about authority and the need to respect it. You do not have to understand or like it, but you must respect it. I am the God of the Universe. Everything on this earth is Mine. However, I need you to trust Me, to develop that muscle of faith.
Take your firstfruits to your church.

*"Honour the Lord with your wealth, with the
firstfruits of all your crops."*
Proverbs 3:9

Tithing

The more I learn about the Kingdom of Heaven—the one that we pray will come to earth every time we recite the Lord's Prayer—the more I see the balances that exist.

To me, tithing is about HONOUR. Honour God with your firstfruits.

PushPay is a New Zealand technology company (GO the KIWIS!) that have created world-class giving solutions. Their mobile technology is used extensively in US churches for tithing, and they created a 2019 Giving Report looking specifically at church giving (have a look at their website).

Here are some of the statistics in that report (https://pushpay.com/blog/church-giving-statistics/):

1.   Less than 25% of regular churchgoers tithe at least 10% of their income.

2.   Religious giving is down about 50% from 1990.

3.   On average, Christians give 2.2% of their income to churches, but during the Great Depression, they gave 3.3%.

So, the Body of Christ is not really resourcing the Body of Christ!

I wonder HOW much more effective the church could be if it was properly resourced?

What impact would we make on our local communities by sharing our huge store of firstfruits with the hungry and the needy, the hurting and the despairing? We could be the hands and feet of Jesus, with no chains of poverty attached!

There are a lot of people who believe that the 10% tithing message is "so Old Testament" and was cancelled out by the return of Jesus. Jesus' call was for us to love one another and to love our neighbours. How can we love people without meeting their material needs before we can address the emotional and spiritual ones? And as a body, how do we resource this if people don't tithe?

The PushPay report also states that lower-income families are more likely to make some form of tithing than higher-income families (who earn over $75,000). In the US, this could be accounted for by the way that tax is structured—once people hit a certain income threshold, the tax bill really ramps up. We don't have that to the same extent in New Zealand.

I would encourage everyone to tithe, and to tithe at least 10% of their income.

I know that, for some people, tithing is almost a financial impossibility. I know that it will not fit into your budget. But then again, let's remember what God Himself says about giving out of the abundance He has blessed you with.

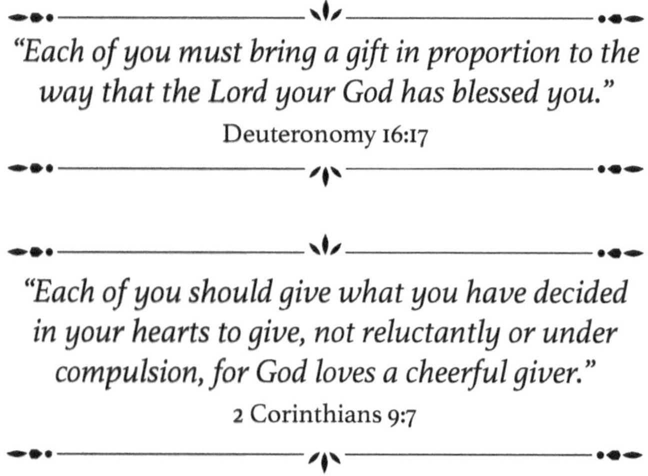

"Each of you must bring a gift in proportion to the way that the Lord your God has blessed you."

Deuteronomy 16:17

"Each of you should give what you have decided in your hearts to give, not reluctantly or under compulsion, for God loves a cheerful giver."

2 Corinthians 9:7

You know what? At the end of the day—at the end of your life—your tithing is between you and God. He knows exactly what money you have coming in and what you do with it. It is a question of honour and also of faith. God rewards faith spectacularly.

Remember the widow in 1 Kings 17? Elijah met her when she was gathering sticks to cook her last meal for herself and her son, after which they would starve to death. Elijah asked her to make the last small loaf of bread and bring it to him on the verbal promise that God would provide her with flour and oil until the rains came. My Bible says that "she went away and did as Elijah had told her".

How would it have looked in her home as she baked the bread? Did she sob as she made the decision to do what Elijah had asked? Did her son tell her that she was nuts and berate her while she made the bread? Was she so defeated and so hopeless that her faith was just the size of a mustard seed? Was she just thinking that it didn't matter, that she was going to die anyway and she may as well roll the dice? How grim might it have been in that home as she followed the word of the prophet.

There is nothing about this that made sense in the natural, but God works in the SUPERNATURAL. God honours those who honour Him (1 Samuel 2:30).

I would encourage you to tithe, because making provision releases provision—it is a biblical principle.

In his commentary about Matthew 20, Matthew Henry says that God is no man's debtor. I also know that God honours those who honour Him with their firstfruits. Clearly the kingdom of God has different supernatural boundaries than New Zealand Financial Planning 101! I have heard stories of people who stepped out in faith and have been provided for (by God) in other ways —free firewood, free meat, free lawnmowers, even free cars! God honours those who honour Him, it's as simple as that, no matter how complicated it looks.

You can sob in your kitchen, you can have people around you tell you that you are nuts. Your faith can be the size of a mustard seed. You may feel defeated and hopeless. But God knows that you are NOT going to be defeated and that there is hope. Share the miracle that you receive with your church. Step out.

"Yet the Lord longs to be gracious to you; therefore He will rise up to show you compassion. For the Lord is a God of justice. Blessed are all who wait for him!"

Isaiah 30:18

MAKE WISE DECISIONS FOR THOSE WHO DEPEND ON YOU

Stewardship is not just about looking after money wisely. It is about making wise choices for those who are dependent on you. You need to make sure that they will be protected and provided for.

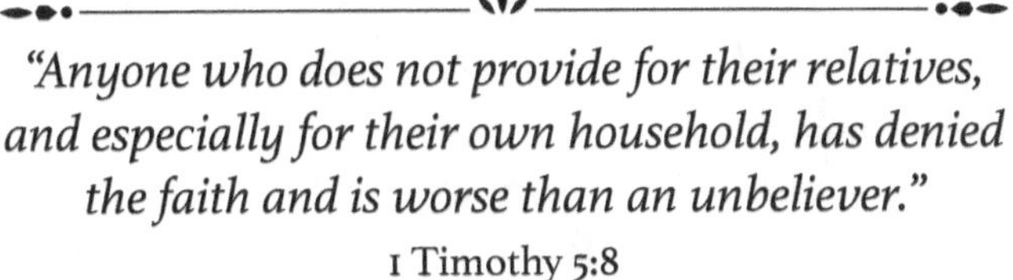

*"Anyone who does not provide for their relatives,
and especially for their own household, has denied
the faith and is worse than an unbeliever."*
1 Timothy 5:8

My Word talks a lot about leaving a legacy. A godly legacy is a heritage of goodness—in the spiritual sense, in the emotional sense and also in the financial sense. It is powerful to live in the legacy of a great man or a great woman. It brings comfort and strength—and they are with Me, praying for you. They want you to build on the work which they started.

In this age, there are legal ways to leave the legacy. You need to make a will, so that your legacy can be passed down to your family in an orderly manner. The widows and orphans need to be provided for; you can buy life insurance for this. These are modern tools for biblical principles. USE THEM.

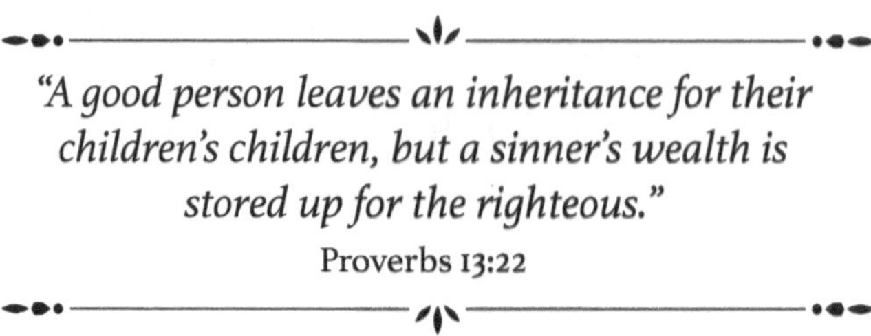

"A good person leaves an inheritance for their children's children, but a sinner's wealth is stored up for the righteous."

Proverbs 13:22

<u>Personal risk protection</u>

Insurance is the concept of pooling your risk with a large group of people, paying your premium to be in the pool, and really hoping that you are not the poor sod who has to call on the promise that you have insured for.

There are instances of "insurance" as far back as the Roman Empire days, where burial clubs existed. You paid in a premium to cover your funeral costs and also some payments to family after you had died.

In the 1700s, widows and orphans funds sprung up in the USA and the United Kingdom. People contributed to these funds, which then paid out small lump sums to women and children who found themselves without a means to survive if their husband or father died and the household income stopped.

The principle is still very much the same. Insurance is about PROTECTING those you love. If the unthinkable happens, and it happens every day to good people, an alternative source of funds needs to be provided so that those you love can manage. If you have taken on the responsibility (and privilege) of raising children, part of your obligations include making financial provision for them.

Let's start with the most basic and common type of insurance: LIFE INSURANCE. This pays out a lump sum if you die or if you are deemed to be terminally ill (which is commonly defined as having less than 12 months to live). It is commonly used to clear mortgage and business debt, pay for funeral and legal expenses and provide money for the ongoing living costs of the people who love you most. This can range from providing a few months off for a spouse to emotionally recover, to providing for multiple years of child support. The premiums are term cover: you pay the premiums each year, and you have the cover. You can increase or reduce the cover to match your financial circumstances, and when you no longer need the cover, you stop paying the premiums.

However, most people don't just die suddenly. The reality is that a lot of them have long periods of ill health before they die, and this is the type of event that takes people out financially. The reality is that it is a hard journey that involves the sick person and everyone around them.

> ## Your income may dry up because you are too sick to go to work, but the costs of living do not stop.

There are still bills to be paid, food to be bought and often multiple medical visits that require transport there and back. The statistics show that one in five working-age adults have six consecutive months off work before they reach the age of 65. That is a very long time! If your income stops fairly early in that six months, you will lose your accommodation—how can you pay rent or service your mortgage with no money? You will not be able to pay for necessities like food, power and transport. You may have to make drastic changes, such as moving in with relatives or borrowing money from family and friends to get through. It is an additional stress on top of other BIG stress. You may qualify for a sickness benefit from Work and Income, but they require you to spend pretty much all of your savings before you qualify for a benefit. You can take a 90-day mortgage repayment holiday if your mortgage is less than 80% of the value of your house, and this will provide some relief, albeit short-term.

This is where people take out INCOME PROTECTION INSURANCE (which involves insuring a percentage of your income) or MORTGAGE INSTALMENT INSURANCE (which covers the mortgage instalments). Yes, it is not cheap insurance and that is because so many people claim on it! However, it sure beats the alternative.

> I cannot tell you how many times clients have said to me that they have no idea how they would have got through severe illness without having this insurance.

It allows them to put all of their energy into focusing on getting through their treatment and recovering. If you are the sole breadwinner or the main income earner and people are depending on you, you really need to look at what you can afford to do in this space. Anything is better than nothing.

There are lots of other types of insurance available, and this is where a good insurance broker with multiple insurance options is worth their weight in gold. You can get insurance that will pay out a lump sum if you become permanently disabled and can't ever go back to work again, either in any job (any occupation) or in your specialised job (own occupation). This is called TOTAL

AND PERMANENT DISABILITY INSURANCE, and is a really useful cover for repaying debt.

You can get a lump sum payment insurance, called TRAUMA COVER, which will pay out a lump sum if you are diagnosed with one of the specified medical conditions which are covered in the policy wording. The main illnesses covered are cancers, heart problems and strokes and these account for the huge majority of the claims. Every policy has cover for different illnesses of varying severity, so once again, it is useful to have a professional who can explain in plain English what you are covered for. A lot of clients use this cover as a top-up for their income cover. It puts a lump sum in the bank to give them a cash buffer as they deal with what is ahead of them.

These are the main insurances that are available in the personal space. There are similar policies available in the business space for business owners to insure for the replacement of key staff, cover business overheads, and provide lump sums in the event of significant illness, total and permanent disability and on death, so that shareholders can pay out other shareholders or their families and the business can continue.

This is equally as important as providing for your family, as other families are dependent on your business to provide for them as well.

Another personal insurance that is widely available in New Zealand is MEDICAL INSURANCE. This can pay for your surgery and your hospital visit, for your specialist costs and medical tests, for your ongoing medical treatment, for your doctor and dentist bills, and for your prescriptions and eye glasses. Obviously, the more that you choose to insure, the more that you pay. Some policies cover drug treatments which are not subsidised by PHARMAC, so you will never need to set up a Give-a-Little page. This type of insurance is really useful for self-employed people as you can schedule your surgery for your quiet time and prepare your business for your absence. In the public system, you have to go when you are called and often have very little notice about this, which can be really difficult to manage. There are also a lot of treatments which are deemed "non urgent" in the public health system but which can be really debilitating. If you are self-employed, you need to be on top of your game at all times, and able to deal with your medical issues quickly.

Medical insurance does not give you a weekly income while you are sick— it just picks up the medical bills.

We do have Accident Compensation in New Zealand, which will pay 80% of your wages if you are injured as the result of an accident. ACC defines as accident as "a specific event which causes an injury to a person". However, cancer is not an accident. A stroke is not an accident. A heart attack is not an accident. If you are injured but there is a pre-existing weakness or a degeneration in the area, ACC will not cover your injury. It doesn't matter whether you knew that you had a pre-existing degeneration or not. Let's face it, as we age, most of us have degeneration in our old bones and ligaments. My poor husband has been on the wrong side of a few ACC decisions as x-rays have shown degeneration in his joints—which he was not aware of and had no symptoms of! Thank goodness for our medical insurance policy, which then picked up the bills for his surgeries. Luckily, he has only had two income protection claims and yes, one of them was for close to six months when he had rotator cuff surgery.

In New Zealand, we have a culture of insuring our houses, our house contents and our cars. Apparently over 90% of Kiwis have some house or contents insurance in place. However, we don't take out any insurance to meet the financial obligations required to KEEP them, and to protect their long term use for your families. That needs to change. Our FAMILIES need to come first, and not our stuff!

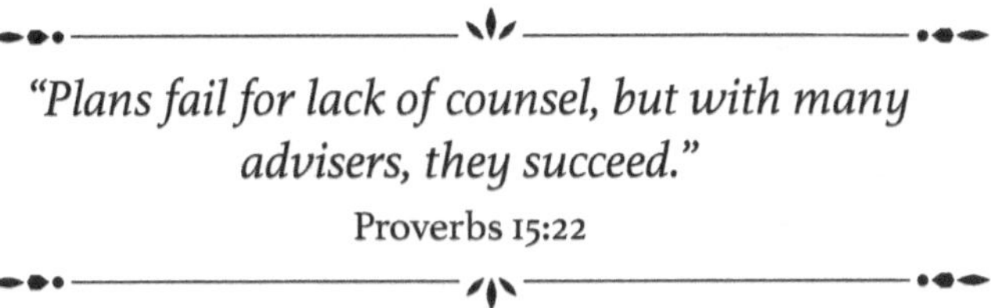

"Plans fail for lack of counsel, but with many advisers, they succeed."
Proverbs 15:22

Estate planning

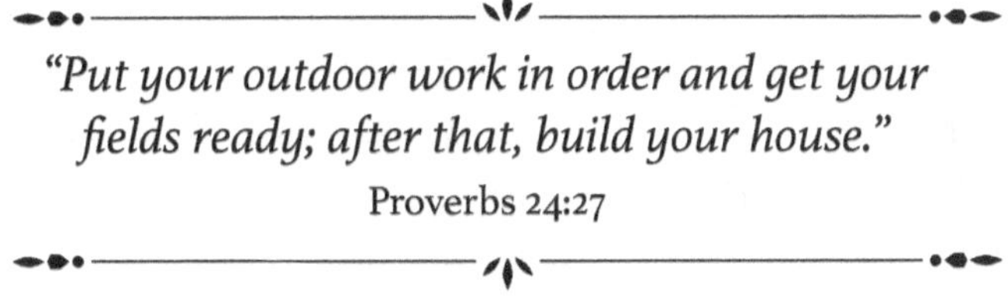

"Put your outdoor work in order and get your fields ready; after that, build your house."
Proverbs 24:27

Having your house in order is very important. Lack of estate planning is an area where negligence can have massive consequences for people who are emotionally involved with or financially dependent on you.

The law of this land (New Zealand) is that, if you have assets in your sole name worth more than $15,000, you are required to have a will.

Most people have this amount in their KiwiSaver. Game on!

Under your will, you appoint executors and trustees. These are the people who will undertake the role of dealing with your assets and distributing them to your beneficiaries. It is a big job. The people that you appoint have to be reasonably smart and be able to do it in a timely manner. If you wish, you can appoint a trustee company (such as Perpetual Guardian Trust) or a solicitor to do the work for your family.

You can specify if you wish to be cremated or buried and give some instructions about your funeral. Just make sure that your family knows that this information is in your will, so they can access the information before they organise your funeral.

You can leave specific gifts to specific people. This can be a cash amount or the gift of a specific item, such as a family heirloom. You can also leave gifts to charities and other organisations.

You will nominate who will receive the residue of your estate – what is left after the payment of the funeral costs, your outstanding bills and the gifts specified under your will. You can specify an age at which a person will receive the money. Under current law, a person cannot be paid an inheritance until they reach the age of 20. If they are under 20, the money has to be held in trust for them and paid out when they reach that age. Your children or grandchildren can however claim for their education or any other financial help which they need which you would have reasonably provided if you were alive.

> If you don't have a will when you die, someone will have to apply to the High Court to have your estate administered under the law of intestacy and to have an administrator appointed.

This is a longer and much more costly process than having made a will.

The law of intestacy also sets out WHO the beneficiaries of your estate are going to be. This may not be how you thought that your assets were going to be divided up. The details of what the split of assets will be is set out here:

https://nzlaw.co.nz/the-closing-chapter/what-if-theres-no-will

Children

The other circumstance where it is ideal to have a will is if you have children under the age of 18. It is a requirement of New Zealand law that all children have a legal guardian if they are under the age of 18. If you die without a will and there are no living birth or adoptive parents for the child, the guardianship has to be determined by the Court. There have been cases where children have been placed into foster homes until guardianship has been determined by the Court. When I worked for a professional trustee, I was involved in one of these cases. It was not a kind process for the little girl in question.

You can appoint custodial guardians who will physically live with your children and look after them on a day-to-day basis and you can appoint testamentary guardians, who will look after the money side of things and ensure that your children's rights and needs are protected. A legal guardian has to be 18 years of age.

Making a will

Having worked for a professional trustee for 13 years, I would strongly recommend that you get legal assistance to make your will. If a will is not drawn up correctly, it will be referred to the High Court for a judgement regarding the interpretation of the will, and legal costs will be incurred. Once again, these will be much higher than what it would have cost you to have a solicitor or trustee company make a will for you in the first place.

A solicitor or trustee company will often store your original will, as the original document has to be produced at the High Court to obtain probate. It is a way of making sure that your will is safe until it is needed.

Yes, sometimes it is difficult to know what (and who!) to put in your will. Yes, sometimes people don't know how to set things up, particularly when there are blended families. This is where getting good legal advice comes in. A good adviser will come up with options and strategies that you didn't even know existed.

Do not leave it until you are sick and preparing to meet your maker. This is NOT a good time to be dealing with things like this. Not everyone gets the chance to prepare to enter Heaven.

Please make your will NOW!

Making an enduring power of attorney

An Enduring Power of Attorney (EPA) is a legal document which appoints someone to step in and take over decision-making for you if you are unable to because you are mentally or physically unwell, are absent (away or overseas) or just don't want to have to manage your affairs yourself any longer.

This is a legal document that is valid only while you are alive. This is the opposite of a will, which only comes into effect when you have died.

There are two types of Enduring Power of Attorney.

The first is called "in relation to Property". This basically means that this document controls your assets—the things that you own. The person or people who have been appointed under this document will step in to pay your bills and look after things for you until you either get well enough to take it over again, or you die.

**If something happens to you
(like an accident or a stroke),
no-one can access assets in your
sole name without an Enduring
Power of Attorney.**

Someone will have to apply to the High Court to have a property manager appointed on your behalf. All interested parties will need to have separate legal representation such as your spouse/partner and your children. The legal costs can easily run into five figures.

If there is no-one logical that you feel that you can appoint, you can appoint a professional trustee company or your solicitor. You can appoint more than one person to act jointly as your Property manager.

Under certain circumstances, your Property EPA holder can act for you in relation to duties that you may have as a company director and as a business owner; but your Property EPA holder cannot act for you as a trustee under a family trust. The other trustees will have to act and appoint a replacement trustee if you are not going to be able to return to your duties as a trustee.

The second is called "in relation to Personal Care and Welfare". The person that you appoint under this document will make important medical decisions for you and will also choose your rest home if needed (so make sure that it is a very nice person!) You can only appoint one person, and a professional trustee cannot act in this role. Once again, if a Personal Care and Welfare EPA is needed and you don't have one, the same process applies as the Property EPA. Most rest homes or private hospitals will not admit patients unless they have a Personal Care and Welfare EPA in place, because this is the person that they have to legally liaise with.

These documents have to be prepared by a solicitor or professional trustee, and the person that you appoint has to get independent legal advice before they sign the document. This ensures that they are aware of what they are taking on, and that they are consenting to act if required.

Family trusts

A family trust is a separate legal entity, just as a company is a separate legal entity. The trust is set up and has an initial asset invested by the settlor. The trustees are the people responsible for operating the trust and making the decisions. The beneficiaries are the people or groups who can benefit from the trust, either while it is running or when the trust is wound up.

> Trusts are really useful for
> protecting assets from being
> claimed on by business creditors or
> by relationship property claims, and
> from being contested when you die.

With changes in Property Relationship Act law, a trust alone will NOT protect your assets from a claim, but it puts another firewall in place (especially if you know how to manage your Property Relationship Act boundaries).

A lot of people set up trusts a long time ago, when they were also useful in avoiding having to pay rest home subsidies. However, with changes to how trusts are viewed, most trusts do not offer that protection any longer.

With regards to having a trust which will stand up to scrutiny from a Court, there are minimum administration requirements for it to be deemed a compliant trust. Trustees must record minutes of any changes to the trust or its assets and must also have an annual general meeting (which needs to be minuted as well).

There have been changes with effect on 30 January 2021 around how trusts are managed and what reporting requirements the trustees will have to provide to beneficiaries going forward.

If you have a trust and you are wondering what to do with it, now is a good time to have it professionally reviewed.

If you choose to wind up a trust that has had taxable income which the trust has declared, please ask your accountant whether there will be any tax clawbacks for winding up the trust and transferring the assets back into the name of individuals.

SUMMARY

- Review your personal insurances— what type of insurance do you have and for what amount?

- What insurance do you not have that you need?

- Do you have a will and is it still appropriate for you?

- Do you have Enduring Powers of Attorney?

- Is your trust compliant with the new trust legislation?

In conclusion

Right from the start of this journey, the Holy Spirit was very clear that this book was to be for followers of Jesus, and for fellow New Zealanders. This is for YOU. For whatever purpose, these words are for YOU. The Holy Spirit has been insistent for 5 years now that this book needed to happen, so here it is—and here you are.

For me, the purpose of this little book is to help you to take power over your financial life, and to give you information to help you to make some informed decisions about what you do.

Some of it will not be easy. I used to belong to a female business owners group and we used to talk about "putting on our big girl pants" when we had to do things or make business decisions that it would have been more pleasant to avoid! Some of this will be the same for you and you will have to put on your "adulting pants" to make the commitment to follow some of these things through.

I really hope that you do, because it truly makes a difference.

Benediction

"This day I call heaven and earth as witnesses against you that I have set before you life and death, blessing and curses. Now choose life, so that you and your children may live and that you may love the Lord your God, listen to His voice and hold fast to Him."
Deuteronomy 30:19-20

May this be a Day of Small Beginnings for you—may this be the day that you start on your journey to financial freedom.

KINGDOM KEYS
for building prosperity

WORKBOOK

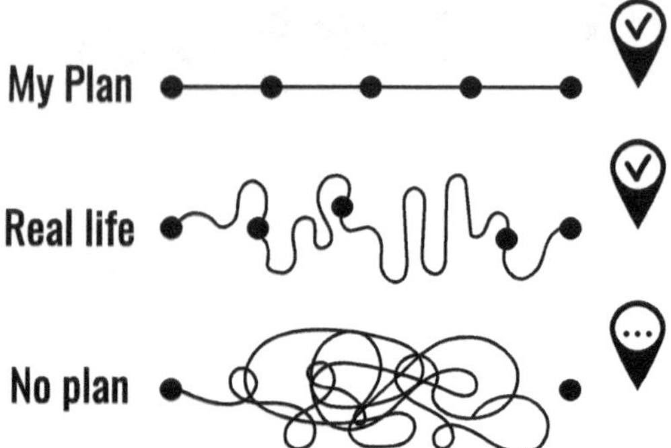

My Plan
Real life
No plan

WORKBOOK

<u>My MOST IMPORTANT VALUES</u>

- ....
  ....
  ....
  ....

- ....
  ....
  ....
  ....

- ....
  ....
  ....
  ....

<u>My FINANCIAL GOALS</u>

University	*New equipment*	*House*
Retirement		*Sport*
Holiday		*Art*
Dream car		*New car*
Missions trip		*Education*
OE		*Help my kids*
Experiences		*Lava glass*
Dental work		*Travel*
Spa pool		*Music concerts*
Bucket list item	*Visit family overseas*	*Shoes*

<u>My SPENDING</u>

Things that I NEED to have:

- Somewhere to live: rent/mortgage
- Food (supermarket)
- Transport (bus/train/petrol/car registration & insurance)
- Phone/Internet to communicate
- Clothes and toiletries
- Utilities: power/rates/insurance
- Tithing

....

....

....

....

Things that I WANT to have:

- Spotify/Apple Music/Netflix/Sky TV/New Faith Network
- Digital subscriptions
- Takeaways
- Hobbies
- Sports equipment
- Movies

....

....

....

....

Analysis of 3 MONTHS SPENDING

<u>My SPENDING PLAN</u>

Does my CURRENT SPENDING match up with my goals and values?

If so, where?

....

....

....

....

If not, where?

....

....

....

....

What do I want to CHANGE?

....

....

....

....

....

....

Spending plan STRUCTURE

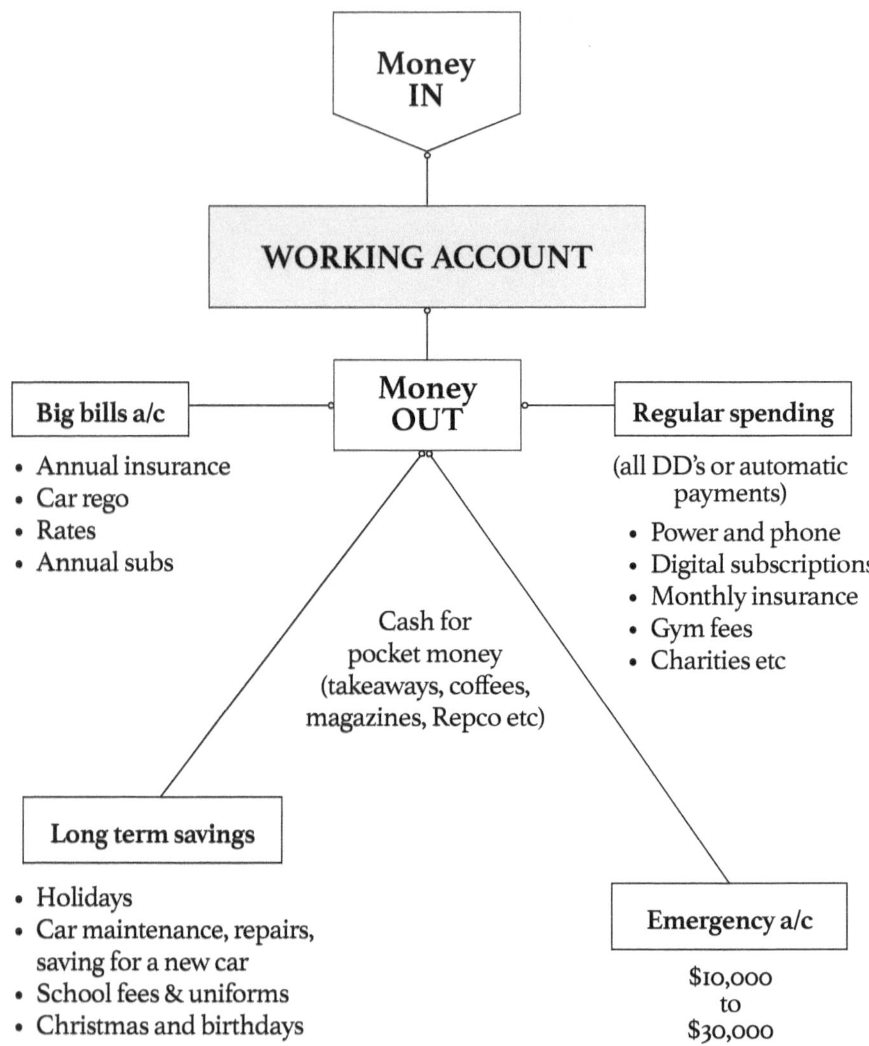

Debt MANAGMENT

What DEBT do I have?

Who with	Balance owing	Interest rate	Payments made	End date

STRATEGY:

1. Target either the smallest one or the highest interest rate.

2. Put ALL your extra money into this one UNTIL
   it has been paid off.

3. CELEBRATE!

4. Take the money you were paying onto this debt,
   and put it onto the next debt and go again.

5. Repeat the above 4 steps until you're DEBT FREE!

Risk <u>MANAGEMENT</u>

Final expenses (funeral & legal) ($5k to $10k) $............................

Repay debt $............................

One years' salary for my partner $............................

Household emergency fund ($5k to $30k) $............................

Education funding for children $............................

Stay at home parent / reduced hours
$........................... per year .... years $............................

Retirement savings top up $............................

Leave a legacy $............................

____

$............................

<u>My WILL</u>

1.   **Who will be the executors and trustees?**

   - Money Smart

   - Time to do it

   - A professional trustee company?

2.   **Do I want to put in funeral instructions?**
   (but let family know as well)

3.   **Guardians for my children**

   - CUSTODIAL guardians for day-to-day care

   - TESTAMENTARY guardians to interact with
     the executors and oversee the money

4.   **Final beneficiaries**

   - Gifts (physical things)

   - Bequests (a gift of a set amount of money)

   - Residual beneficiaries (who gets what is left)

<u>KIWISAVER</u>

What asset allocation to use?

1. How long before I will access the money—
    first home buyer / retirement

2. How tolerant am I of the investment market
    ups and downs?

**Complete an investor risk profile such as the one on
www.sorted.org under the guides/saving and investing tab.**

What provider to use?

1. Active vs passive management

2. Fees vs performance (always look at the 10 year
    performance as your starting point)

How much to save?
Start high and ease back if you need to.